DATE DUE			
SEP - 3 2002			
OCT 0 5 2002			
6/30			
MAY 1 7 2004			
DEC 1 4 2004			
JUN 1 9 2005			
OCT 1 8 2005			
FEB 2 4 2006			
JAN 2 5 2008			
SEP 2 2008			
DEC 0 6 2017			

FROM THE DINOSAURS OF THE PAST TO THE BIRDS OF THE PRESENT

MARIANNE JOHNSTON

The Rosen Publishing Group
PowerKids Press
New York

Published in 2000 by The Rosen Publishing Group, Inc.
29 East 21st Street, New York, NY 10010

First Edition

Book Design: Michael de Guzman, Resa Listort, Danielle Primiceri

Photo Credits: p. 3 © Linda Hall Library, Kansas City and © Stockbyte; p. 4 © Stockbyte; p. 6 © Linda Hall Library, Kansas City and © John Taylor/FPG International; p. 8 © Telegraph Colour Library/FPG International; p. 10 © Stockbyte, © Tom McHugh/National Museum of Natural History, and © Peabody Museum; p. 12 © Linda Hall Library, Kansas City; p. 14 © Linda Hall Library, Kansas City and © Chris Butler/Science Photo Library; p. 16 © Joe Tucciarone/Science Photo Library; p. 19 © Chris Butler/Science Photo Library; p. 20 © O. Louis Mazzatenta/National Geographic Image; p. 22 © Stockbyte.

Johnston, Marianne.
    From the dinosaurs of the past to the birds of the present / by Marianne Johnston.
       p.   cm. — (Prehistoric animals and their modern-day relatives)
    Includes index.
    Summary: Describes the evolution of dinosaurs and birds and discusses how the two groups may be related.
    ISBN 0-8239-5204-5
    1. Dinosaurs—Juvenile literature. 2. Birds, Fossil—Juvenile literature. 3. Birds—Juvenile literature. [1. Dinosaurs. 2. Birds, Fossil. 3. Birds. 4. Prehistoric animals.] I. Title. II. Series: Johnston, Marianne. Prehistoric animals and their modern-day relatives.
    QE862.D5J66 1998
    567'.9—dc21

                                      98-3880
                                         CIP
                                       AC

Manufactured in the United States of America

Contents

There's a Dinosaur in My Backyard!

What would you do if your little brother ran into the house and said, "Hey, I just saw a dinosaur"?

You'd laugh, right? Well, think again. Your little brother might not be making it up.

Many scientists believe that right now, the relatives of dinosaurs are alive and well. Just step outside and look in the sky or in a nearby tree. If you see a bird, you may be looking at the relative of a dinosaur!

Many scientists think that all the dinosaurs died about 65 million years ago. This book will tell you how one kind of dinosaur may have **evolved** into today's birds.

◄ *Not only do many scientists believe that birds came from dinosaurs, some even call birds "living dinosaurs."*

REIGN OF THE DINOSAUR

The **prehistoric** dinosaurs lived on Earth for 165 million years. Scientists have found **fossils** from over 450 different kinds of dinosaurs.

Stegosaurus, with its sharp tail spikes and armored back plates, lived 170 million years ago.

A dinosaur called **diplodocus** lived around the same time. It was almost as long as three school buses parked end to end! Diplodocus loved to stretch its long neck into the trees to eat tasty leaves.

Large, powerful dinosaurs like this Stegosaurus with its baby, ruled Earth until about 65 million years ago. ▶

Saltopus lived 220 million years ago. This dinosaur was smaller than a house cat. Saltopus had long legs for running and short arms for grabbing his food.

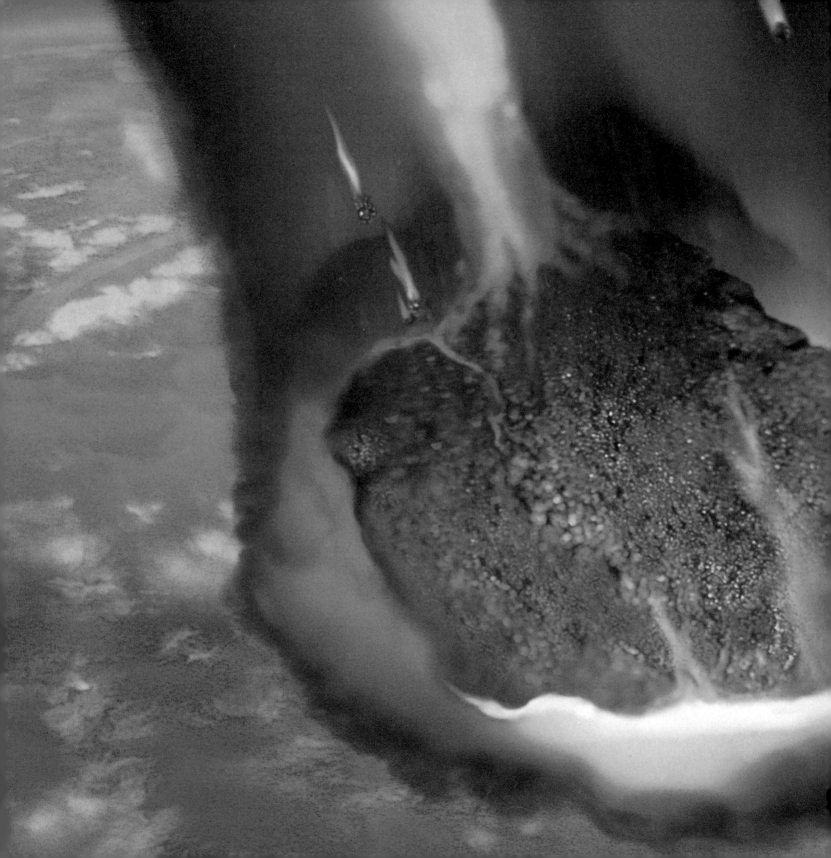

WHY DID MOST OF THE DINOSAURS DIE?

Scientists believe that a huge comet or **asteroid** crashed into Earth about 65 million years ago. They think that this six-mile-wide space object caused a huge crater in the Gulf of Mexico.

Some scientists also believe that at the same time the asteroid crashed, a huge volcano erupted in what is now India.

Both of these events probably sent tons of smoke and dust into the **atmosphere**. The dust and smoke blocked out sunlight for months all over Earth.

Scientists say that the change in the atmosphere from one or both of these events probably killed off most of the dinosaurs.

There are many explanations for why the dinosaurs died out. But today, the asteroid idea is the one most scientists believe.

EVOLUTION

The very first dinosaurs lived about 225 million years ago. Over millions of years, the dinosaurs that came from these **ancestors** went through a slow process of change called **evolution**. Different types of dinosaurs with different **characteristics** began to develop. The dinosaurs with characteristics that helped them survive lived for a long time. The dinosaurs with characteristics that didn't help them died out.

This process of evolution happened for the creatures that live on Earth today. Scientists believe that even people have gone through evolution. They believe that humans came from the same ancestor as the apes.

It takes millions of years for one type of animal to evolve into another.

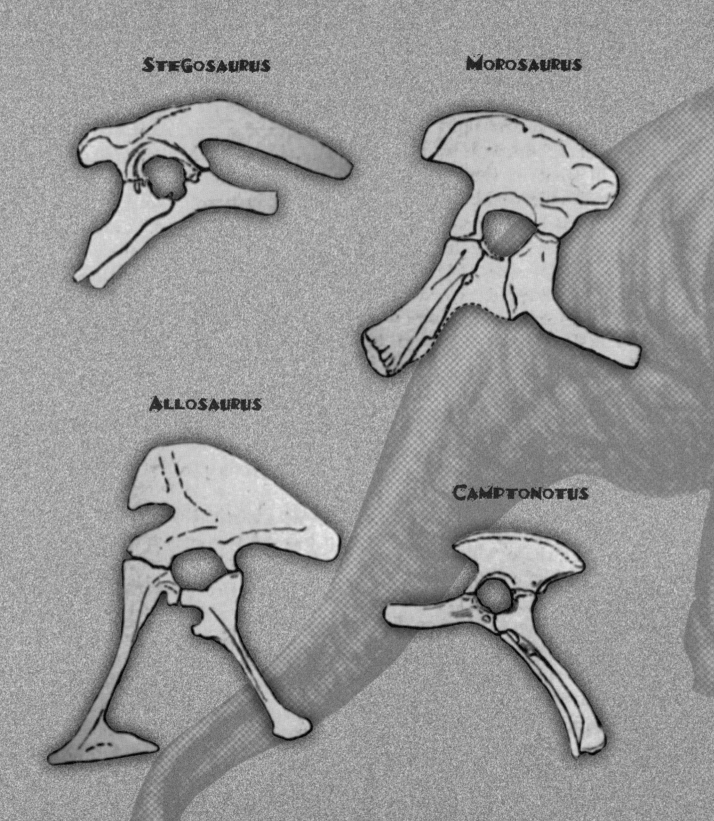

STEGOSAURUS

MOROSAURUS

ALLOSAURUS

CAMPTONOTUS

Studying Bones

Scientists look closely at the **similarities** between different animals. This helps them decide which animals are related to one another. Scientists study prehistoric animal and dinosaur bones this way.

When scientists first looked at birds to figure out what they may have evolved from, they saw some amazing things. They discovered that birds have a lot in common with dinosaurs. All dinosaurs had a hole in their hip **socket**, where the leg bone connects to the main part of the body. And birds have the same hole! This led scientists to believe that birds and dinosaurs may be related.

No matter how different the rest of a dinosaur's body may be from that of another dinosaur's, chances are their hip sockets are the same.

Hollow Bones

Did you know that the bones of birds are hollow? Well, guess what other animal had hollow bones? **Tyrannosaurus rex**. This enormous meat-eating dinosaur was a type of dinosaur called a **theropod**. All dinosaurs in the theropod family had hollow bones.

For a long time, scientists thought that birds had developed hollow bones so that their bodies would be lighter for flying. But now we know that hollow bones were around in dinosaurs long before birds ever existed!

A scientist named John Ostrom was the first scientist to compare bird-like fossils to those of theropods. ▶

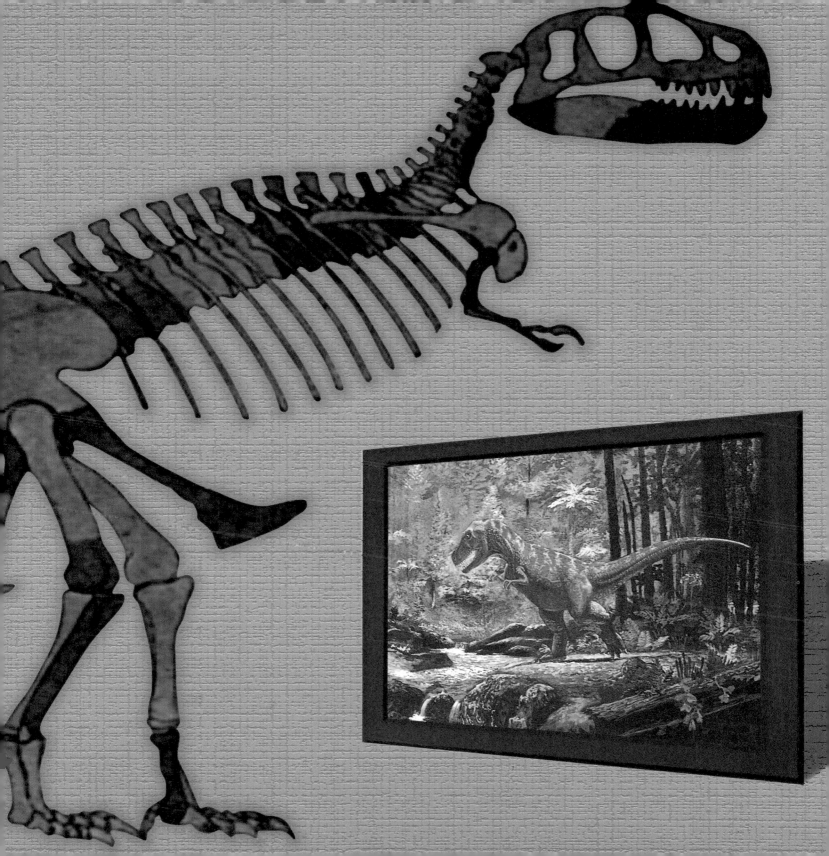

Another Clue

The theropods came in all shapes and sizes. One group that evolved from those hollow-boned dinosaurs was the **maniraptors**.

Maniraptors had a special bone in each wrist that was shaped like a half-moon. I bet you can guess which kind of animals today have this same wrist bone. That's right—birds do!

So far, we have three major clues that birds are related to dinosaurs:

- Birds have the same hip socket that all dinosaurs had.
- Birds have hollow bones like theropods had.
- Birds have a special wrist bone like maniraptors had.

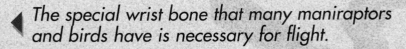

The special wrist bone that many maniraptors and birds have is necessary for flight.

CLOSE RELATIVES OF THE FIRST BIRD

Two close relatives of the first bird were maniraptors. **Velociraptor** was a maniraptor that was about six feet long, and about three feet tall. It ran quickly and close to the ground as it chased its **prey**. Long, sharp claws, made for catching prey, grew from the hands and feet of velociraptor.

Another maniraptor, called **deinonychus**, grew to be twelve feet long. This dinosaur hunted the same way that velociraptor did. They looked alike too.

Both of these dinosaurs had a certain bone in the center of their chests called a wishbone, just like most modern birds do.

Velociraptor and deinonychus were quick at catching prey, much like today's hawks and eagles are. ▶

This fossil of Protarchaeopteryx (which shows traces of feathers) is very important in studying the evolution of dinosaurs to birds.

▼

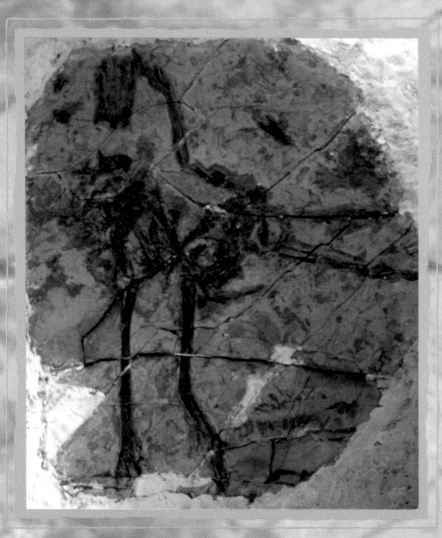

A New Discovery!

   Scientists have recently made exciting discoveries in China. They found fossils of dinosaurs that had feathers. Some of the fossils found are of **caudiopteryx**. This animal was one of the first to have feathers, but it probably couldn't fly. Fossils of another feathered creature, called **protarchaeopteryx**, have also been found in China. This dinosaur had longer feathers than caudiopteryx, but couldn't fly either. Caudiopteryx and protarchaeopteryx probably had feathers to keep warm.

   The most famous bird-like animal is **archaeopteryx**. It lived about 150 million years ago. Archaeopteryx had jaws and teeth instead of a beak. But archaeopteryx had feathers that were much like the feathers of today's bird. Archaeopteryx probably used those feathers to keep warm and maybe to fly very short distances. Archaeopteryx is believed to be the first bird.

ARCHAEOPTERYX TO BIRD

Scientists are becoming more convinced that dinosaurs led directly to today's birds. Scientists have found fossils in Spain of a creature that probably came after archaeopteryx that more closely resembles a bird.

This creature, called **eoalulavis**, had a special group of feathers, called an **alula**, attached to its thumb. These feathers are on today's birds and are very important. These feathers allow birds to control takeoff and landing.

Discoveries are made every day. Scientists are more sure than ever that the dinosaurs from long ago are the direct ancestors to the seagulls, crows, and parrots that fly around Earth today.

WEB SITE:

www.tyrellmuseum.com/home.html

Glossary

alula (AL-yoo-luh) A tuft of feathers on a bird's wing where its thumb would be.

ancestor (AN-ses-ter) A creature from which others evolve.

archaeopteryx (ar-kee-OP-tuh-riks) The earliest known bird.

asteroid (AS-teh-royd) A rock that orbits other larger objects in space.

atmosphere (AT-mus-feer) The layer of gases surrounding Earth.

caudiopteryx (KAW-dee-OP-ter-iks) One of the first dinosaurs to have feathers.

characteristic (KAR-ak-tuh-RIS-tik) A quality that makes a person or thing unique.

deinonychus (dyn-ON-ih-kus) A maniraptor that is a close cousin of the first bird.

diplodocus (dih-PLUD-oh-kus) A huge plant-eating dinosaur that lived 170 million years ago in what is now the western part of the United States.

eoalulavis (ee-OL-yoo-LAY-vis) The first modern bird.

evolution (eh-vuh-LOO-shun) A slow process of change and development that living things go through over many, many years.

evolve (ee-VOLV) To develop and change over many, many years.

fossil (FAH-sul) The hardened remains of a dead plant or animal.

maniraptor (MAN-ih-rap-ter) A type of dinosaur that developed into the common ancestor of archaeopteryx and modern-day birds.

prehistoric (pree-his-TOR-ik) Happening before recorded history.

prey (PRAY) An animal that is eaten by other animals for food.

protarchaeopteryx (proh-TAR-kee-OP-ter-iks) One of the first dinosaurs to have feathers.

saltopus (sal-TOP-us) A tiny dinosaur that lived 220 million years ago.

similarity (sih-muh-LAR-ih-tee) A characteristic that is the same as someone or something else's.

socket (SAH-kit) An opening or hole meant to hold something.

stegosaurus (steg-uh-SOR-us) A dinosaur that grew to be thirty feet long and had an armor-like outer skin. It lived in what is now the western part of the United States.

theropod (THEHR-uh-pod) A type of dinosaur that had hollow bones like modern birds.

tyrannosaurus rex (tih-RA-nuh-SOR-us REKS) A huge meat-eating theropod that lived about 90 million years ago.

velociraptor (veh-LAH-suh-rap-ter) A maniraptor that is a close cousin of the first bird.

INDEX